THE
MAGNIFICENT
BOOK OF
PREHISTORIC
BEASTS

THE
MAGNIFICENT
BOOK OF
PREHISTORIC
BEASTS

ILLUSTRATED BY
Val Walerczuk

WRITTEN BY
Tom Jackson

weldon**owen**

Written by Tom Jackson
Illustrated by Val Walerczuk

weldon**owen**

Published by Weldon Owen Children's Books
An imprint of Weldon Owen International, L.P.
A subsidiary of Insight International, L.P.
PO Box 3088
San Rafael, CA 94912
www.insighteditions.com

Weldon Owen Children's Books:
Designer: Anna Pond
Senior Editor: Lydia Halliday
Consultant: Darren Naish

Insight Editions:
CEO: Raoul Goff
Senior Production Manager: Greg Steffen

ISBN: 979-8-88674-065-3

Printed in China.
First printing, July 2024. RRD0724

10 9 8 7 6 5 4 3 2 1

MIX
Paper | Supporting
responsible forestry
FSC® C144853

Introduction

Let's take a look at some magnificent prehistoric creatures. All the creatures included in this book lived on Earth for millions of years, but they are now all extinct. In other words, every one of them has died out completely, and we will never see them alive again. So how do we know about them? All the answers are found in fossils, which are rocks that have formed from the remains of long dead animals. Scientists use fossils—of bones, shells, and even feathers—to figure out what ancient animals looked like. Sometimes they might disagree on what they looked like, but there is usually a common interpretation. There are at least one million animal species living today, but fossil scientists have found that the number of extinct animals could add up to 100 million! Prehistoric creatures are just as amazing as today's animals—perhaps even more so. You will find a woolly mammoth, a relative of elephants that was covered in thick fur, a saber-toothed cat with teeth as long as your arm, and a shark with a mouth big enough to walk around inside. Older prehistoric animals look like nothing you've seen before: *Tiktaalik* was a fish that could walk, *Arthropleura* was a millipede bigger than a man, and *Anomalocaris* was a 500-million-year-old hunter that had eyes on stalks and ate food through a tube. Read on for all this and more. Have a magnificent time!

Fact file

Lived: North Africa, Europe, North America

Meaning of name: Dunkle's bones

Length: 33 ft (10 m)

Weight: 1.1 tons (1,000 kg)

When: 370–360 mya

Diet: Sharks and other large fish

Contents

Andrewsarchus

- *Andrewsarchus* is the largest meat-eating land mammal of all time.

- The only fossils of *Andrewsarchus* are of its huge skull, but this tells scientists that this giant animal was related to hoofed animals like hippos and cows. Scientists are uncertain whether they had hooves or claws, or something in between.

- No hoofed animal living today is a meat-eater, but *Andrewsarchus* had sharp teeth for slicing meat.

- As well as sometimes killing animals, *Andrewsarchus* was probably mainly a scavenger. Its jaws were strong enough to crush the bones and shells of the dead animals it found.

Fact file

Lived: East Asia

Meaning of name: Andrew's beast

Length: 18 ft (5.5 m)

Weight: 1.1 tons (1,000 kg)

When: 40–35 mya

Diet: Meat

🐻 *Andrewsarchus* is thought to be a relative of today's whales and dolphins, which also evolved from hoofed land animals.

🐻 This creature is named after Roy Chapman Andrews, an American fossil hunter and explorer, who is said to be the inspiration for the movie character Indiana Jones.

🐻 *Andrewsarchus* might have lived alone and only met other members of the species to mate or during fights over food.

Megalodon

- *Megalodon* was the largest type of shark ever to swim in the world's oceans.

- Like all sharks, *Megalodon* did not have a bony skeleton. Only a few fossil teeth and fragments of spine have been found.

- This shark's mouth was more than 6½ ft (2 m) wide, meaning it could swallow an adult man whole.

- *Megalodon* had dozens of saw-edged teeth that were around 6 in (15 cm) long—that's bigger than an average man's hand.

Fact file

Lived: Oceans worldwide

Meaning of name: Big tooth

Length: 53 ft (16 m)

Weight: 52 tons (48,000 kg)

When: 16–1.6 mya

Diet: Whales and other sea creatures

Like today's great white shark, *Megalodon* hunted in deep water and surged upwards at great speed to grab prey from underneath.

 Megalodon would take a few bites to kill large prey such as a whale. Its first bites would target the tail and flippers to stop its victims from swimming away.

 Megalodon could only swim in warm water. It perhaps became extinct because most large whales began living in cold polar waters, where the shark could not hunt.

Mammuthus primigenius

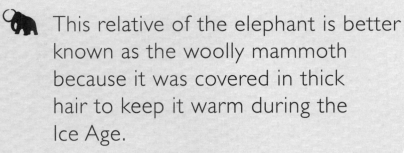 This relative of the elephant is better known as the woolly mammoth because it was covered in thick hair to keep it warm during the Ice Age.

The mammoth used its curved tusks to scrape the snow from the ground to reveal food.

This mighty beast could go without food for days on end. It stored a supply of energy in the hump between its shoulders.

Fact file

Lived: North America, northern Europe, Siberia

Meaning of name: Burrower

Height: 11¼ ft (3.4 m)

Weight: 6.6 tons (6,000 kg)

When: 4.8 million–4,000 years ago

Diet: Grass, moss, lichens, bark

The woolly mammoth had much smaller ears than today's elephants. The skin on big, floppy ears would have frozen in the cold.

Mammoths sometimes got stuck in mud and were covered by snow, becoming frozen solid for thousands of years.

Early fossil hunters who found buried mammoths thought that the woolly beasts had dug themselves burrows.

The last surviving group of woolly mammoths lived on an Arctic island. These mammoths were dwarfs at only 6 ft (1.8 m) tall.

Arthropleura

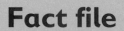 *Arthropleura* was a giant relative of today's millipedes. It was the largest land arthropod to have ever lived.

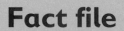 The animal had 120 legs and scuttled through swampy forests, leaving tracks 20 in (50 cm) wide.

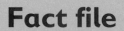 *Arthropleura* had no natural enemies—it could lift the front of the body up to scare away any other animals that came too near.

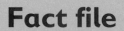 The main food of *Arthropleura* was plants, but it was also a scavenger and ate dead bodies.

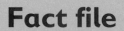 *Arthropleura* lived at the time when the first trees appeared on Earth, forming huge forests. It became extinct when these forests died away.

Fact file

Lived: Europe, Asia, North America

Meaning of name: Side joints

Length: 8½ ft (2.6 m)

Weight: Unknown

When: 340–280 mya

Diet: Plants and animals

- The arthropod was perhaps able to grow to its large size because the air in the Earth's atmosphere contained more oxygen at the time.

- *Arthropleura* had to shed its hard skin from time to time as it grew.

Arctodus

Also known as the short-faced bear, this animal had much longer legs than today's bears.

The closest living relative to the short-faced bear is the spectacled bear of South America.

Like today's bears, this giant beast could stand on its back legs—and reach up to 14 ft (4.3 m) with its arms—that's twice as high as the world's tallest people.

Despite its long legs, the short-faced bear could not run fast for very long. However, it could walk for days on end without needing a rest.

The short-faced bear probably stole food from smaller predators by using its huge size to scare them away.

The bear needed to eat at least 35 lb (16 kg) of meat everyday to survive—that's the equivalent of a whole sheepdog!

The short-faced bear had a larger nose than today's bears and could sniff out dead bodies to scavenge from many miles away.

Fact file

Lived: North America

Meaning of name: Bear tooth

Length: 6 ft (1.8 m)

Weight: 1 ton (900 kg)

When: 1.8 million–11,000 years ago

Diet: Animals and plants

Bos primigenius

- Also known as the aurochs, this was the wild relative of today's cattle.

- Aurochs had very long, forward-curving horns that reached up to 30 in (80cm) long.

- Aurochs lived in small herds in winter, but roamed woodlands and grasslands by themselves in summer.

- The first farm cattle were bred from aurochs living in India about 9,000 years ago. All of the world's cattle are descended from them.

- The closest living wild animal to the aurochs is the gaur, which lives in the forests of southeast Asia.

- The last wild aurochs ever recorded died in Poland in 1627.

Fact file

Lived: Europe, Asia, North Africa

Meaning of name: Original bull

Length: 6 ft (1.8 m)

Weight: 1.65 tons (1,500 kg)

When: 2 mya–1627 CE

Diet: Grass

Archelon

- This ancient reptile was the largest turtle that ever lived. Its shell was almost as wide as it was long.

- *Archelon* lived in a warm, shallow sea that covered the center of what is now North America.

- Males stayed at sea for their whole lives, and females only came on land for a few hours each year to lay eggs on beaches.

- The turtle had no teeth but used its horny beak to crush its food, which included shellfish and squid.

- The giant shell was covered in a leathery skin which stretched over a framework of ribs, and so was not as heavy as it looked.

Fact file

Lived: North America

Meaning of name: Large turtle

Length: 15 ft (4.5 m)

Weight: 2.43 tons (2,200 kg)

When: 75–65 mya

Diet: Jellyfish, ammonites, other shellfish

Archelon's nearest living relative is the leatherback turtle—which is the largest living species.

The front flippers of the turtle measured nearly 16½ ft (5 m) from tip to tip. That made the turtle as long as a family car, but twice as wide.

Hatzegopteryx

Hatzegopteryx was a giant pterosaur—a flying reptile that lived at the time of the dinosaurs.

This reptile was one of the largest flying animals of all time. Its wings were as large as those on a four-seater airplane.

To get into the air, experts think that *Hatzegopteryx* had to run fast along the ground. It then soared high in the air, riding on upward currents of warm air.

Hatzegopteryx could stay in the air for 10 days at a time while looking for prey!

When it found prey, this monster flyer swooped down and grabbed it in its long, pointed jaw.

Hatzegopteryx could also walk on all fours with is wings folded out of the way.

It is likely that *Hatzegopteryx* also scavenged on the bodies of dead animals that they saw while flying.

Fact file

Lived: Eastern Europe

Meaning of name: Hateg wing (named after the Hateg Basin in Romania)

Wingspan: 36 ft (11 m)

Weight: 550 lb (250 kg)

When: 72–66 mya

Diet: Dinosaurs

Diplocaulus

- *Diplocaulus* was an amphibian and a distant relative of salamanders and frogs.

- This fish-eater lived in water throughout its life, although it could walk over land for short distances.

- *Diplocaulus* had a curved arrow-shaped head. Biologists are uncertain as to why the head was this shape.

- Its wide head was made of solid bone and may have made *Diplocaulus* difficult for large predators to swallow. Most prehistoric beasts could not chew and so swallowed their meals whole.

Fact file

Lived: North America

Meaning of name: Double helmet

Length: 3¼ ft (1 m)

Weight: 10 lb (4.5 kg)

When: 298–250 mya

Diet: Fish

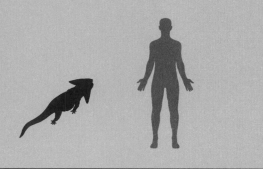

Diplocaulus's head may have also worked like a wing, making it easier for the animal to stay afloat. It is also thought to have been used in combat and to attract mates.

Diplocaulus skimmed along the surface, using its long flattened tail to push through the water.

Diprotodon

- *Diprotodon* was the largest marsupial (an animal that raises babies in a pouch) to ever live.

- *Diprotodon* was a relative of today's wombats and koalas but was the size of a rhinoceros.

- This giant beast was a plant-eater that lived in woodlands. It used its large front teeth to bite through tough plant stems.

- *Diprotodon* was still living in Australia when the first Aboriginal people came to live there. It is suggested that the mythical Australian monster, called a bunyip, is based on this creature.

Fact file

Lived: Australia

Meaning of name: Two forward teeth

Length: 9¾ ft (3 m)

Weight: 2.75 tons (2,500 kg)

When: 1.8 mya–40,000 years ago

Diet: Grass, roots, leaves

🐾 Despite being large, the *Diprotodon* was at risk of attack from giant crocodiles and lizards that lived in Australia at the time.

🐾 It is thought that male *Diprotodons* fought each other using their huge front paws as they competed for mates.

🐾 The animal had strong claws on its flat feet, which it used for digging up roots to eat.

Doedicurus

Doedicurus was a giant relative of today's armadillos.

This car-sized beast was covered in a dome of armor which protected it from all attackers.

The armor shield was made from small plates of bone that were linked together, so the covering was more flexible than it looked.

Doedicurus's main enemies were giant meat-eating "terror birds." It defended itself with the spikes on the tip of its tail.

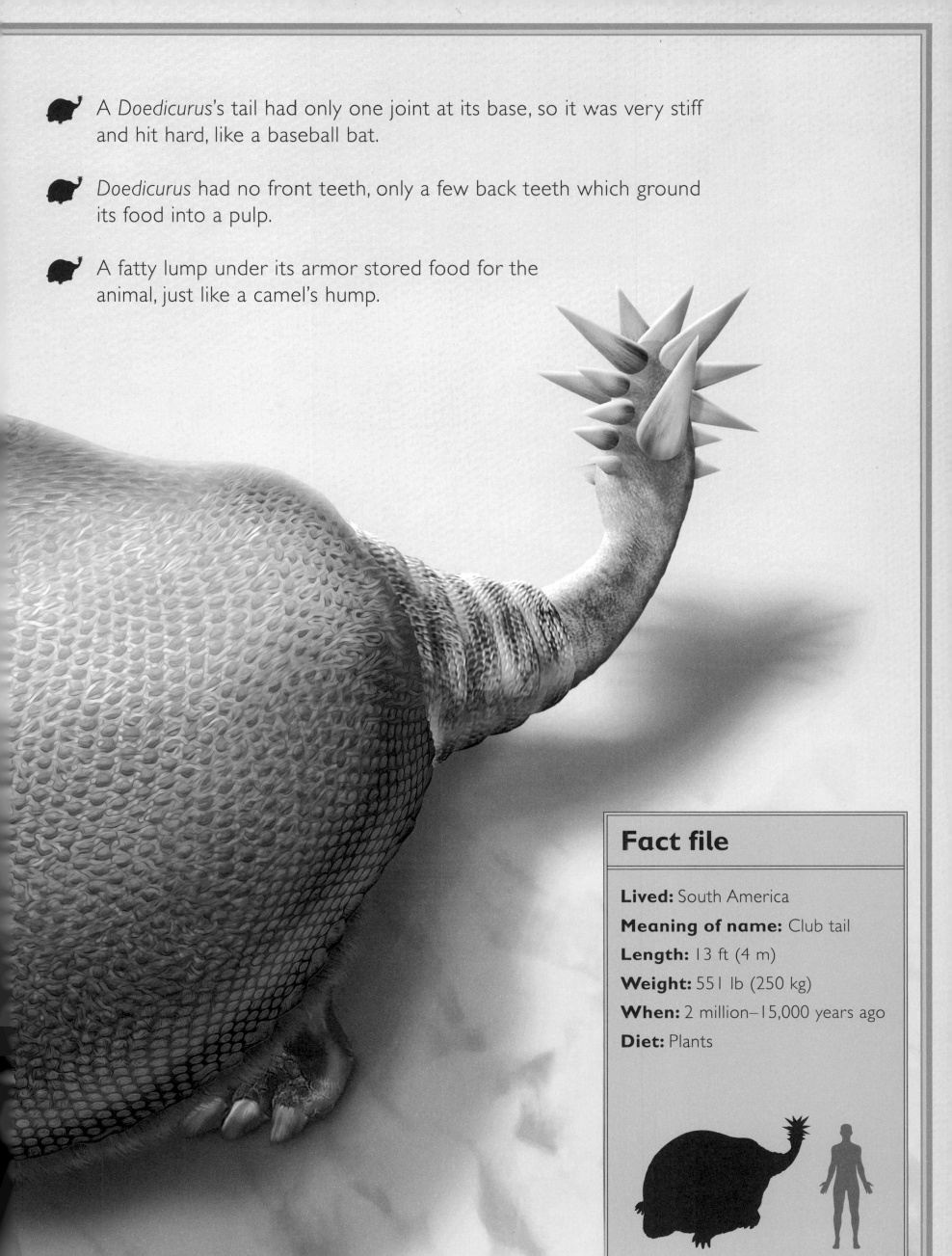

- A *Doedicurus*'s tail had only one joint at its base, so it was very stiff and hit hard, like a baseball bat.

- *Doedicurus* had no front teeth, only a few back teeth which ground its food into a pulp.

- A fatty lump under its armor stored food for the animal, just like a camel's hump.

Fact file

Lived: South America

Meaning of name: Club tail

Length: 13 ft (4 m)

Weight: 551 lb (250 kg)

When: 2 million–15,000 years ago

Diet: Plants

Ambulocetus

- *Ambulocetus* was an ancestor of today's whales that lived in rivers and along the coast of southern Asia.

- *Ambulocetus* hunted like a crocodile. It hid in shallow water and grabbed victims that came close with its long, powerful jaw.

- *Ambulocetus* was a powerful swimmer, but unlike today's whales, it had legs and could walk over dry land.

- This hunter used its tail and back legs to power through the water and steered with its webbed feet.

Fact file

Lived: South Asia

Meaning of name: Walking whale

Length: 9¾ ft (3 m)

Weight: 660 lb (300 kg)

When: 50–49 mya

Diet: Meat

While whales and dolphins evolved from *Ambulocetus*, this creature's ancestors were large meat-eating hoofed animals like *Andrewsarchus*.

 Ambulocetus could hear well underwater but not in air. On land the animal pressed its jaw against the ground to pick up tiny vibrations from animals moving nearby.

 Ambulocetus killed its prey by pulling them into the water so they drowned. It then ate the prey underwater.

Entelodon

- *Entelodon* was a rhino-sized creature that looked like a warthog or wild pig. However, it was not a relative of today's pigs.

- *Entelodon* had a huge head. Its skull made up about a third of its total body length.

- Its long snout was filled with big teeth. Fossil specimens often contain broken or worn-down teeth, which suggests *Entelodon* chewed bones.

- *Entelodon* was a scavenger, and would eat whatever it found, from fallen fruits to the remains of dead animals.

Fact file

Lived: North America and Asia

Meaning of name: Perfect toothed

Length: 8¼ ft (2.5 m)

Weight: 1.1 tons (1,000 kg)

When: 45–25 mya

Diet: Dead animals, fruit, nuts, roots

Bony lumps, or warts, grew out of the *Entelodon*'s face. They were used to protect the face from bites during fights.

Fossil footprints show that *Entelodon* lived in small groups, probably a male, a female, and their children.

Entelodon had long legs for trotting great distances as it sniffed out food in dry habitats.

Hallucigenia

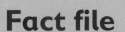 This weird creature is one of the earliest animals known to live on Earth.

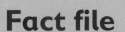 It lived in the sea more than 500 million years ago when most living things were still tiny microorganisms, like bacteria.

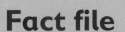 *Hallucigenia* had a body shaped like a worm with spikes and tentacles growing out of it.

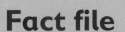 Fossil experts think the animal may have walked on its tentacles and used the spikes for protection.

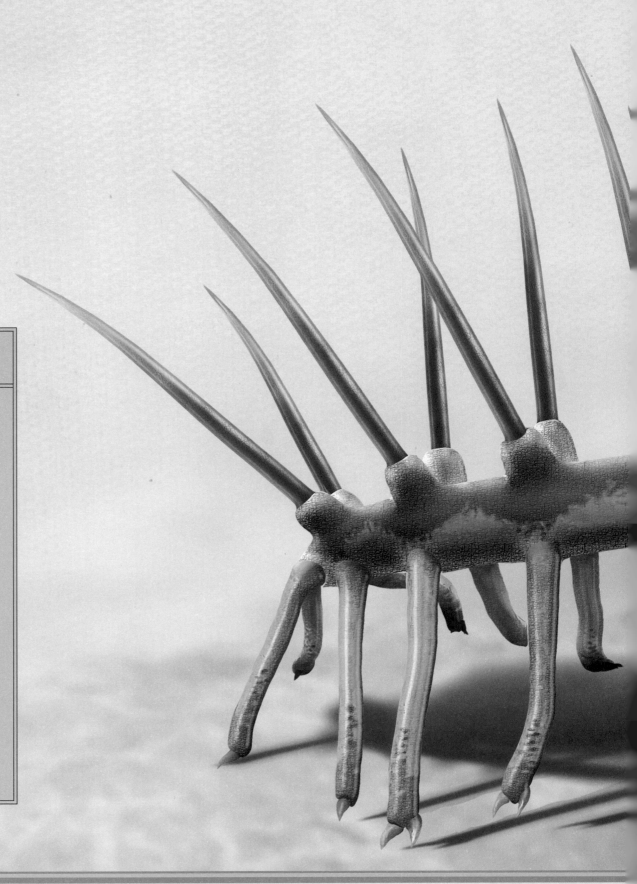

Fact file

Lived: Canada

Meaning of name: Daydream maker

Length: 1¼ in (30 mm)

Weight: Unknown

When: 541–510 mya

Diet: Unknown

- Wormlike animals lived at the same time as *Hallucigenia*, but this creature is one of the first to have what look like legs.

- *Hallucigenia* may be a distant relative of arthropods—animals including crabs, insects, spiders, and centipedes.

- Another theory is that *Hallucigenia* lived the other way up. The spines were used to grip the seabed, and the tentacles waved in the water grabbing passing food.

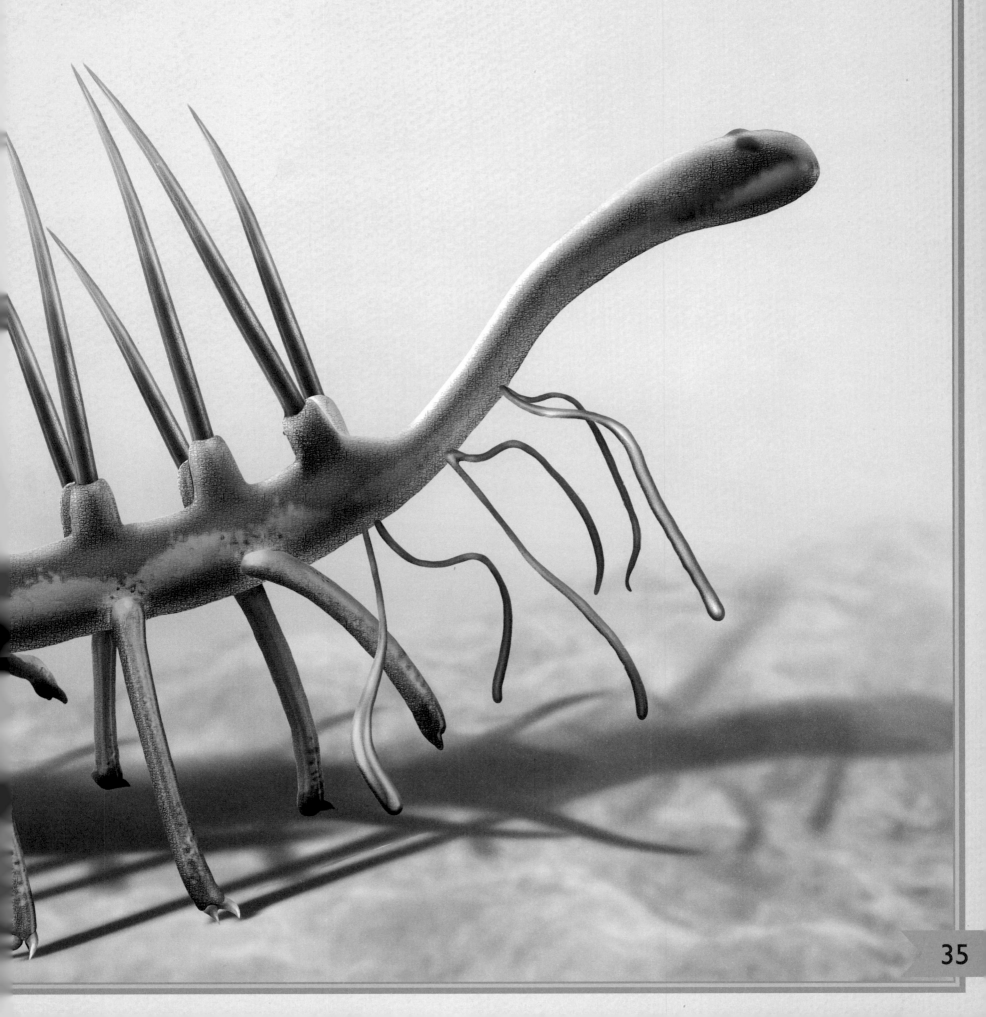

Eohippus

🐎 *Eohippus* is one of the earliest ancestors of the horse—and the donkey and zebra, too.

🐎 It was much smaller than its living relatives, about the same size as a dog.

🐎 *Eohippus* lived in dense forest, eating leaves and fruits that grew on shrubs.

🐎 It was not a fast runner like a horse, but being small it could easily dash out of sight if danger approached.

🐎 A horse's foot has a hoof, but *Eohippus*'s feet were different. They had four toes on the front feet and three at the back.

Fact file

Lived: North America, Europe

Meaning of name: Dawn horse

Length: 2 ft (60 cm)

Weight: 20 lb (9 kg)

When: 56–34 mya

Diet: Leaves, fruits, shoots

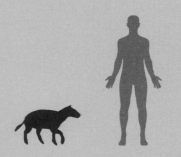

🐾 *Eohippus*'s descendants evolved into horses because the world became drier and the forests turned to open grasslands, where it was safer to be a large, fast runner.

🐾 Some experts suggest that *Eohippus* was also the ancestor of the rhinoceros.

Panthera leo spelaea

- This relative of today's lions lived in Europe and western Asia, and preyed on horses, deer, woolly mammoths—and humans!

- This beast is better known as the cave lion because most of its fossils were found in caves—not because it always lived in caves.

- Cave lions lived in cold forests and the open plains of the Ice Age. In winter, the cave lion's coat would have turned whiter to help it hide in snow.

- The cave lion was a little larger than today's African lion, and it had a thicker coat of hair, so its mane was less obvious.

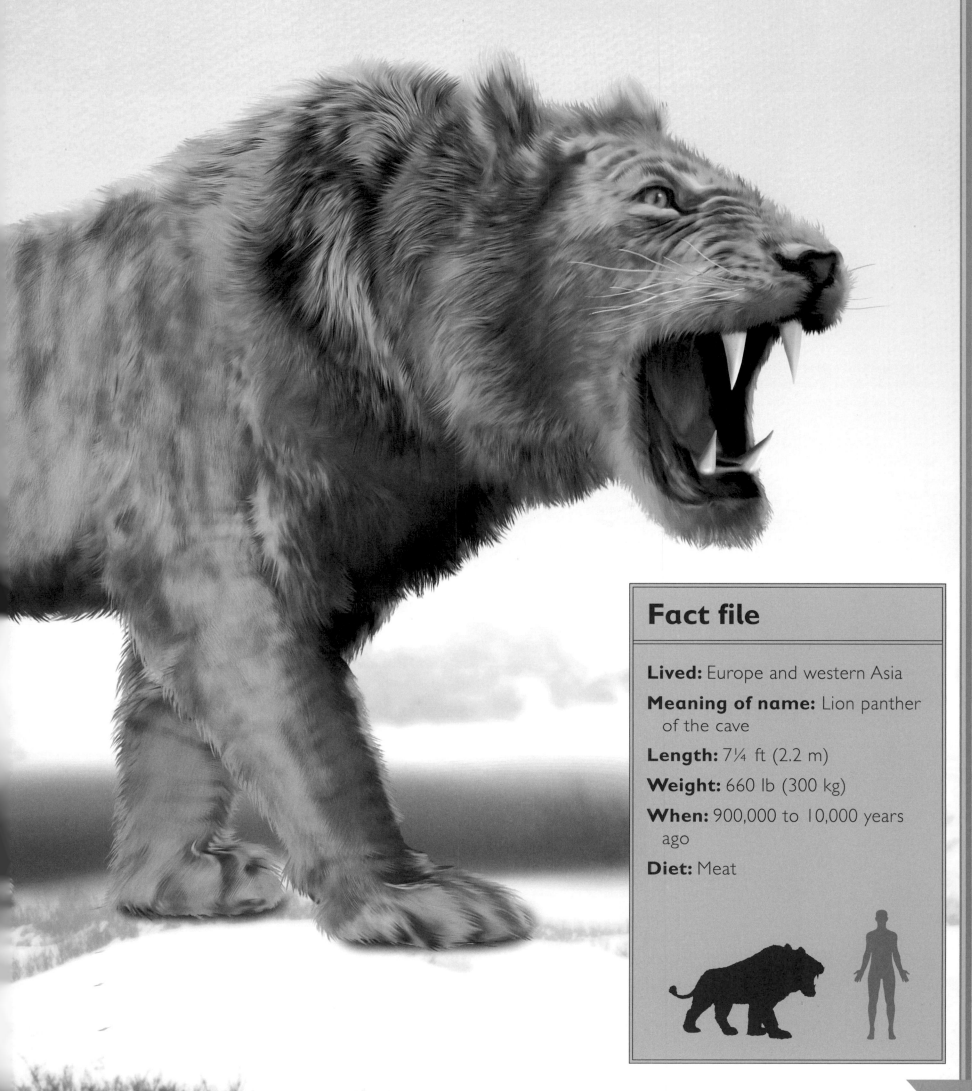

Cave lions hunted alone or in pairs, unlike today's lions, which normally hunt in a larger team.

Cave lions became extinct because wolves took over their territory as the world warmed up.

Fact file

Lived: Europe and western Asia

Meaning of name: Lion panther of the cave

Length: 7¼ ft (2.2 m)

Weight: 660 lb (300 kg)

When: 900,000 to 10,000 years ago

Diet: Meat

Trilobite

- Although they looked a lot like woodlice, *Trilobites* were in fact a completely different group of animals that lived in the sea until about 250 million years ago.

- *Trilobites* were hugely varied in size but they all had a series of plates across their backs, which created a flexible armor.

- A few *Trilobites* could swim, but most lived on the seabed where they dug for prey in the sand or ate seaweeds.

- *Trilobites* had many legs. Most of these were used for walking, but the legs also had feathery gills attached, which took oxygen from the water.

Fact file

Lived: Worldwide

Meaning of name: Three lobes

Length: ¼–32½ in (5 mm–80 cm)

Weight: 10 lb (4.5 kg)

When: 520–252 mya

Diet: Plants and animals

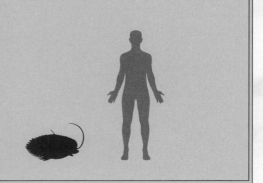

A *Trilobite* had no chewing mouthparts. Instead it ground its food up using spikes that stuck out of its front legs.

Trilobites became extinct in the Great Dying, a mass extinction that killed 96 percent of all life in the seas. Nobody knows what caused it.

The nearest living relatives to *Trilobites* are thought to be horseshoe crabs. Despite their name, these strange animals are not closely related to other crabs.

Gigantopithecus

Fact file

Lived: China, India, Southeast Asia

Meaning of name: Giant ape

Length: 9¾ ft (3 m)

Weight: 1,190 lb (540 kg)

When: 13 million to 500,000 years ago

Diet: Bamboo

- *Gigantopithecus* was the largest ape ever to live on Earth.

- Very few fossils of parts of *Gigantopithecus* have been found, but experts have figured out how large it was from its jaw bones and teeth.

- The first *Gigantopithecus* fossil was a huge tooth found among Chinese medicines in 1935.

- These enormous apes lived in forested hills. It has been suggested that they survived longest in the Himalayan mountains and possibly could be behind the myth of the Yeti, or Abominable Snowman.

- The closest living relatives of *Gigantopithecus* are orangutans, and so experts believe that these giant apes had long red hair as well.

- Although no leg bones have ever been found, it is thought *Gigantopithecus* was too large to climb trees and spent time on the ground.

- The female *Gigantopithecus* was half the size of the male.

Paraceratherium

- *Paraceratherium* was the largest land mammal ever, heavier than an elephant and taller than a house.

- *Paraceratherium* was not quite as tall as today's giraffes—but was much heavier. Like the giraffe, *Paraceratherium* had a long neck to reach leaves at the tops of trees.

- These immense leaf-eaters browsed small trees—one tree had only enough food for one *Paraceratherium* at a time.

- *Paraceratherium* stayed out of the sun on hot days by seeking shade under tall trees.

Fact file

Lived: East India, China, Mongolia

Meaning of name: Near horned beast

Height: 14¾ ft (4.5 m)

Weight: 16.5 tons (15,000 kg)

When: 30–25 mya

Diet: Leaves

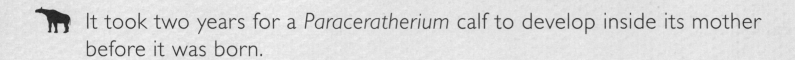 It took two years for a *Paraceratherium* calf to develop inside its mother before it was born.

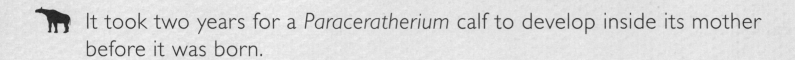 Being so large helped the animal store reserves of water and fat to survive long periods without food.

Pterygotus

- *Pterygotus* was an example of a sea scorpion, an ancient type of hunter that lived on the seabed.

- The creature was one of the largest arthropods to ever live. An arthropod is an animal with an outer skeleton and jointed legs.

- *Pterygotus* is a distant relative of today's spiders and scorpions.

- *Pterygotus* had plates of armor covering its back and had a paddle-shaped tail.

Fact file

Lived: Worldwide

Meaning of name: Winged animal

Length: 9 ft (2.8 m)

Weight: 55 lb (25 kg)

When: 420–410 mya

Diet: Fish and sea creatures

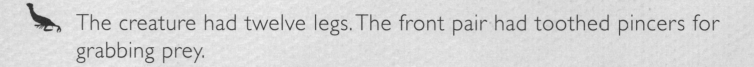 The creature had twelve legs. The front pair had toothed pincers for grabbing prey.

The sea creature swam using its wide tail and a pair of oar-shaped back legs.

It hunted by ambushing prey, burying itself in the sand and lying in wait for fish and other creatures to swim past.

Megalania

- *Megalania* was the largest lizard that has ever existed—bigger even than today's Komodo dragon.

- *Megalania* was an ambush hunter, lying hidden in the bushes and leaping out to grab its prey.

- This giant lizard would have tried to attack and eat some of the first humans who arrived in Australia about 50,000 years ago.

- *Megalania* killed prey by biting their necks with its powerful jaws and hooked teeth.

- When fresh food was hard to find, the monster lizard looked for dead bodies to eat.

- The lizard could kill any animal in Australia, and even attacked prey that were 10 times its own size.

- *Megalania* could run very fast, but for only a short distance before it got too hot and had to stop to cool down.

Fact file

Lived: Australia

Meaning of name: Great ripper

Length: 18 ft (5.5 m)

Weight: 1,320 lb (660 kg)

When: 1.6 mya–40,000 years ago

Diet: Marsupials such as wombats and kangaroos

Liopleurodon

- Experts used to think that this ocean reptile was the largest hunting animal of all time. They thought it might have been as big as an airliner. Now it is known to be only the size of a bus.

- *Liopleurodon* hunted in the shallow seas that covered much of Europe 150 million years ago.

- A large *Liopleurodon* could kill a crocodile, *ichthyosaur* (a dolphin-like reptile), and a big shark.

- *Liopleurodon*'s long jaw was filled with needle-shaped teeth that gripped slippery prey in the water.

- Like a shark today, *Liopleurodon* had a very sensitive nose and could smell prey in the water well before it was close enough to see them.

Fact file

Lived: Europe

Meaning of name: Smooth-sided teeth

Length: 23 ft (7 m)

Weight: 2 tons (1,814 kg)

When: 160–155 mya

Diet: Fish, ichthyosaurs, other marine reptiles

Liopleurodon was a pliosaur, which were giant ocean reptiles with huge heads, a thick neck, and four flippers instead of legs.

Liopleurodon never came on land although they breathed air and had to come to the surface between dives.

Megaloceros

 Megaloceros was a giant deer with the largest antlers in history.

 From tip to tip, the antlers were 12 ft (3.65 m) wide—that is twice the length of a standard bed.

 The antlers were made of 88 lb (40 kg) of bone, and the male deer grew a new set each year.

 The antlers were too large for fighting with regularly. Instead, they were used to impress females and scare off attackers.

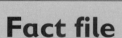 *Megaloceros* lived during the last Ice Age, when being large helped animals to keep warm and survive.

 Megaloceros is often called the Irish elk because it was most common in Ireland where there were fewer predators.

 It is thought that early humans hunted *Megaloceros* to extinction.

Fact file

Lived: Europe, western Asia

Meaning of name: Giant horn

Length: 9¾ ft (3 m)

Weight: 1,230 lb (600 kg)

When: 1.5 million–11,000 years ago

Diet: Grass and herbs

Cameroceras

- *Cameroceras* was an example of an orthocone, a type of giant shellfish that looks like a sea monster from legends.

- Orthocones were an early form of cephalopod mollusc. Today's cephalopods include squids and octopuses.

- *Cameroceras* was the biggest hunter in the Ordovician period, which was a time before large vertebrates (animals with backbones) had evolved.

- This hunter had eyes but relied more on its sense of smell to find prey.

- *Cameroceras* had eight tentacles for grabbing food. The tentacles had grooves on them to grip slippery, struggling prey.

- This giant shellfish moved using a jet of water pumped through a flexible tube. The tube stuck out of its shell and could be pointed in any direction.

- Early fossil hunters believed that the smaller orthocone shells they unearthed were the horns of unicorns.

Fact file

Lived: North America

Meaning of name: Chambered horn

Length: 36 ft (11 m)

Weight: 900 lb (410 kg)

When: 470–440 mya

Diet: Shellfish, trilobites, crustaceans

Megatherium

Megatherium is an extinct relative of the sloth. Instead of living in trees though, this giant lived on the ground.

Megatherium was a little larger than today's elephants.

This giant beast stood up on its back legs to reach leaves and other food high in trees.

Megatherium had long claws on its front paws to hook around branches and pull leaves down to its mouth.

Fact file

Lived: South America

Meaning of name: Great beast

Length: 20 ft (6 m)

Weight: 4 tons (4,000 kg)

When: 1.9 mya–8,000 years ago

Diet: Leaves and fruit

The huge creature had a long, flexible tongue for wrapping around twigs and ripping off the leaves.

Ancient South American people hunted this beast. One *Megatherium* would have fed an entire village!

Megatherium lived in dry woodlands and it became extinct after South America became a much wetter place with more rain.

Smilodon

- *Smilodon*, which means "double-edged knife tooth," is the scientific name for the more commonly known saber-tooth cat.

- The saber-tooth cat's teeth could be as long as 10 in (25 cm).

- Although its teeth were its most famous asset, they were actually very brittle, and could break easily.

- It used to be thought that their teeth were used to grab and hold on to prey, but it is more likely that they were used to deliver the killing blow.

- The saber-tooth cat was around the same size as modern-day lions, but it was much more robustly built.

- The saber-tooth cat could open its mouth very wide, like a snake. This was most likely to keep its long teeth out of the way while it was eating.

- Previously known as the saber-tooth tiger, the saber-tooth cat is only distantly related to modern-day tigers.

- The way that the saber-tooth cat's throat bones were made up suggests that they communicated by roaring, like modern-day big cats.

Fact file

Lived: North and South America

Meaning of name: Double-edged knife tooth

Length: 6½–8¼ ft (2–2.5 m)

Weight: 660 lb (299 kg)

When: 10,000 BCE

Diet: Deer, bison, camels, woolly mammoths

Dunkleosteus

- *Dunkleosteus* was the top predator during the Devonian period, a time when nearly all animals still lived in the oceans.

- *Dunkleosteus* shared the oceans with early sharks, which were its main food.

- This giant fish did not have teeth but its mouth was lined with sharp, bony blades that gave it a powerful bite.

- *Dunkleosteus* could not chew and had to swallow chunks of food whole—and often choked on its food. Scientists have found the fossilized sick of *Dunkleosteus*!

Fact file

Lived: North Africa, Europe, North America

Meaning of name: Dunkle's bones

Length: 33 ft (10 m)

Weight: 1.1 tons (1,000 kg)

When: 370–360 mya

Diet: Sharks and other large fish

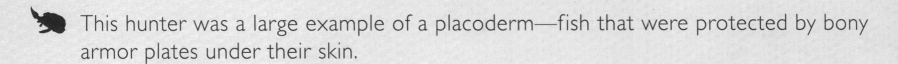 This hunter was a large example of a placoderm—fish that were protected by bony armor plates under their skin.

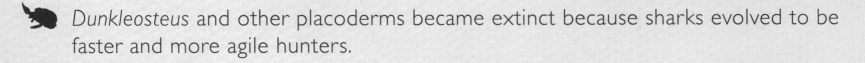 *Dunkleosteus* and other placoderms became extinct because sharks evolved to be faster and more agile hunters.

The fish was named in honor of David Dunkle, a famous American fossil expert.

Brontothere

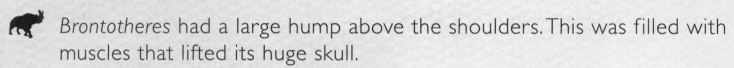 The *Brontotheres* were giant beasts that looked a little like rhinos, but it is thought that they were more closely related to horses.

Brontotheres had a pair of horns growing out of their snouts.

Unlike rhino horns, which are made from the same material as hair, a *Brontothere*'s horns were made of bones growing out of the skull.

Brontotheres lived in herds, and the males used their horns to fight each other over females.

Brontotheres had a large hump above the shoulders. This was filled with muscles that lifted its huge skull.

Fact file

Lived: North America

Meaning of name: Thunder beast

Length: 16½ ft (5 m)

Weight: 3.6 tons (3,300 kg)

When: 56–34 mya

Diet: Leaves, grass

A *Brontothere* had flexible lips and a long tongue for plucking the freshest leaves from shrubs.

Brontotheres became extinct because the shrubs and small trees they relied on for food died out as the world became drier. This was due to climate change.

Thylacoleo

- Also known as the marsupial lion, *Thylacoleo* had one of the strongest bites of any mammal.

- *Thylacoleo* was a marsupial, like a kangaroo, and its babies lived inside a pouch on the mother's belly.

- *Thylacoleo* probably hunted alone, waiting on low tree branches for prey to pass by underneath.

- During an attack, this mighty marsupial leaped on to its victim's back, pulling it to the ground with vicious bites and slashes.

Fact file

Lived: Australia

Meaning of name: Pouched lion

Length: 4 ft (1.2 m)

Weight: 287 lb (130 kg)

When: 3 million to 30,000 years ago

Diet: Animals

This hunter had huge back teeth that slid past each other, cutting in the same way as a pair of scissors.

The claw on the inside toe of the *Thylacoleo*'s front paws was very long and may have been used for slicing open the stomachs of its prey.

Thylacoleo's living relatives include wombats and koalas.

Tiktaalik

- This big fish lived in shallow rivers and pools, and used its huge mouth to gobble up smaller prey.

- *Tiktaalik* could swim, but it also walked on the riverbed using its four bony fins.

- Biologists believe that *Tiktaalik* and fish like it were the ancestors of the first four-legged land animals—that includes all frogs, reptiles, birds, and mammals!

- *Tiktaalik* had gills and could breathe underwater, but it also had small lungs for breathing air when the water ran out of oxygen.

Fact file

Lived: North America

Meaning of name: Freshwater fish

Length: 6½ ft (2 m)

Weight: 50 lb (22.5 kg)

When: 375 mya

Diet: Meat and fish

This fish had nostrils on the top of its snout and its eyes looked upward like a crocodile's. This suggests that *Tiktaalik* grabbed land animals when they came to the water's edge to drink.

Tiktaalik was able to crawl over dry land for short distances as it looked for new bodies of water to feed from.

Fish do not have a neck and cannot move their heads from side to side, but *Tiktaalik* was able to turn its head so it could grab prey better.

Titanoboa

- This monster snake was the largest species of snake ever. It evolved after the dinosaurs died out to be one of the main hunters in South America.

- It lived in tropical rainforests, which were forming for the first time in South America.

- When *Titanoboa* was slithering around, Earth was about 50°F (10°C) warmer than it is now, and it rained twice as much as well.

- *Titanoboa* lived in shallow rivers. It was easier to move its immense body through water than over land.

- The snake killed prey by constriction, wrapping its body around victims and squeezing them so that they could not breathe.

Fact file

Lived: South America

Meaning of name: Titanic boa

Length: 46 ft (14 m)

Weight: 1.25 tons (1,135 kg)

When: 60–58 mya

Diet: Fish, crocodiles

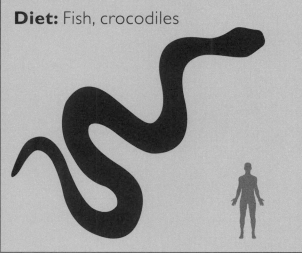

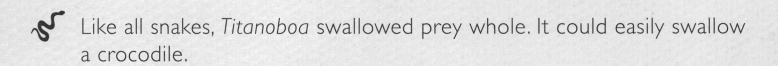Like all snakes, *Titanoboa* swallowed prey whole. It could easily swallow a crocodile.

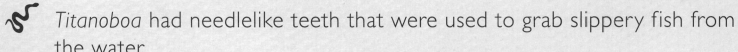*Titanoboa* had needlelike teeth that were used to grab slippery fish from the water.

Gastornis

Fact file

Lived: Europe, North America

Meaning of name: Gaston's bird

Length: 7¼ ft (2.2 m)

Weight: 1.1 tons (1,000 kg)

When: 56–41 mya

Diet: Plants

Gastornis was an ambush hunter. It hid among the shrubs of forests and jumped out on small mammals that walked past. Scientists that discovered *Gastornis* assumed the monster bird must be a fierce killer, but today we know it ate mostly plants.

Gastornis was the heaviest bird to ever live, and some scientists think it was not a high-speed runner. However, other experts suggest they could hit 30 mph (50 kmh), which is faster than a human sprinter.

Gastornis is named after Gaston Planté, a French scientist who discovered early fossils. Later the giant creature was nicknamed the "terror bird."

The terror bird could not fly. Its long, shaggy feathers would have been better for keeping the bird dry and warm, and would have helped it stay out of sight, too.

Gastornis had a massive beak made of thick bones. This gave the bird a strong bite for cracking nuts. It may have ripped off meat from the remains of dead animals, too.

Terror birds such as *Gastornis* became extinct after large, powerful mammals evolved to take their places.

Hesperornis

- This giant diving bird had only tiny wings and so could not fly.

- The seabird lived out at sea all year round and only came on land to lay eggs.

- *Hesperornis*'s body was too heavy for it to stand upright on land. Instead it slithered over rocks and slid up beaches on its belly.

- The bird spent most of its time floating on the surface of the water and made short dives into shoals of fish.

- *Hesperornis* grabbed slippery prey in its long, pointed beak. It returned to the surface to swallow the food whole.

Fact file

Lived: North America

Meaning of name: Western wing

Length: 5 ft (1.5 m)

Weight: 88 lb (40 kg)

When: 80–65 mya

Diet: Fish and ammonites

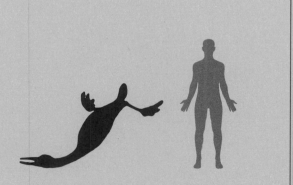

- The bird swam using its wide feet and used its little wings and flat tail to steer.

- Its short, fluffy feathers trapped air bubbles against its skin, making it easier for the bird to float.

Coelodonta

- Also known as the woolly rhinoceros, this huge plant-eater lived in cold grasslands around the edge of the Arctic during the Ice Age.

- As well as a thick fur coat, woolly rhinos had short legs and small ears, leaving them less exposed, which stopped them suffering from the cold.

- Their two nose horns, which were made from a mass of fused hairs, were used to dig out food under the snow.

- Woolly rhinos were drawn in ancient cave paintings in countries where rhinos no longer live.

Fact file

Lived: Northern Europe, Siberia, Asia

Meaning of name: Hollow tooth

Length: 10¾ ft (3.3 m)

Weight: 2.2 tons (2,000 kg)

When: 1.8 million to 20,000 years ago

Diet: Grass, leaves

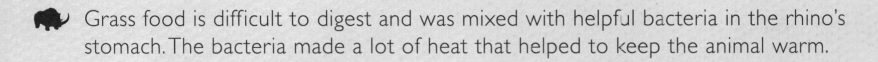 Grass food is difficult to digest and was mixed with helpful bacteria in the rhino's stomach. The bacteria made a lot of heat that helped to keep the animal warm.

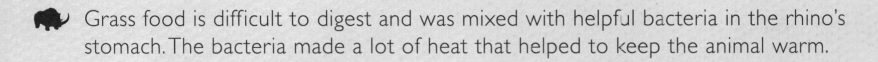 Their woolly fur was waterproofed with wax and oil. The hairs trapped air next to the skin, which stopped body heat from escaping.

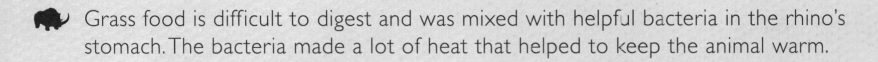 Woolly rhinos became extinct mostly because the world warmed up, which melted much of their habitat. Hunting by ancient people and disease helped to wipe out any that remained.

Anomalocaris

* This weird creature was the largest animal in the Cambrian period. This was a time when the number and variety of animals began to increase very fast.

* *Anomalocaris* looked very different to anything living today. It had a boat-shaped body and swam using a frill of flaps that ran along each side.

* *Anomalocaris* had only a short gut, which tells scientists it ate animals, not plants.

* It had two flexible tentacles, which were lined with spikes. It used the tentacles to snatch prey from the water.

* *Anomalocaris* had a soft body and would not have been able to crush the hard shells of prey. It is thought that it held prey in its mouth and used its flexible tentacles to prise open the shells.

Fact file

Lived: North America, eastern Asia, Australia

Meaning of name: Odd shrimp

Length: 6½ ft (2 m)

Weight: 20 lb (9 kg)

When: 535–520 mya

Diet: Animals

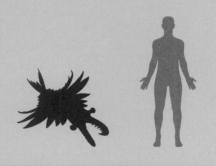

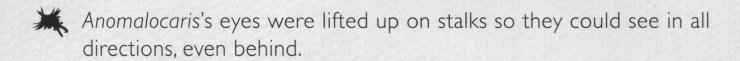 *Anomalocaris*'s eyes were lifted up on stalks so they could see in all directions, even behind.

 Its mouth was a circular tube lined with sharp plates, looking a bit like the surface of a pineapple. The plates crushed food as it was swallowed.

Harpagornis

- This giant bird is also known as Haast's eagle, after the Dutch scientist Julius von Haast, who discovered it in 1871.

- Haast's eagle was the largest eagle to have ever lived, and was almost twice the size of today's eagles.

- It is thought that Haast's eagle was too heavy to fly far. It watched for prey from tall trees or cliffs, and then swooped in for the kill.

- Its main prey was the now extinct moa, tall flightless birds that were even taller than ostriches.

Fact file

Lived: New Zealand

Meaning of name: Hook bird

Wingspan: 9¾ ft (3 m)

Weight: 33 lb (15 kg)

When: 1.8 mya–1400 CE

Diet: Flightless birds, humans

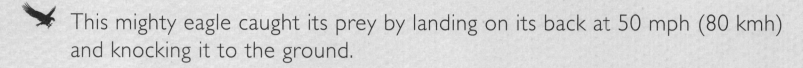 This mighty eagle caught its prey by landing on its back at 50 mph (80 kmh) and knocking it to the ground.

It killed using its long talons, which were as big as a tiger's claws, to crush the neck. It then used its hooked beak to rip off flesh.

The eagle may have possibly attacked Maori people, the first human settlers to live in New Zealand, and ate them slowly over a few days.

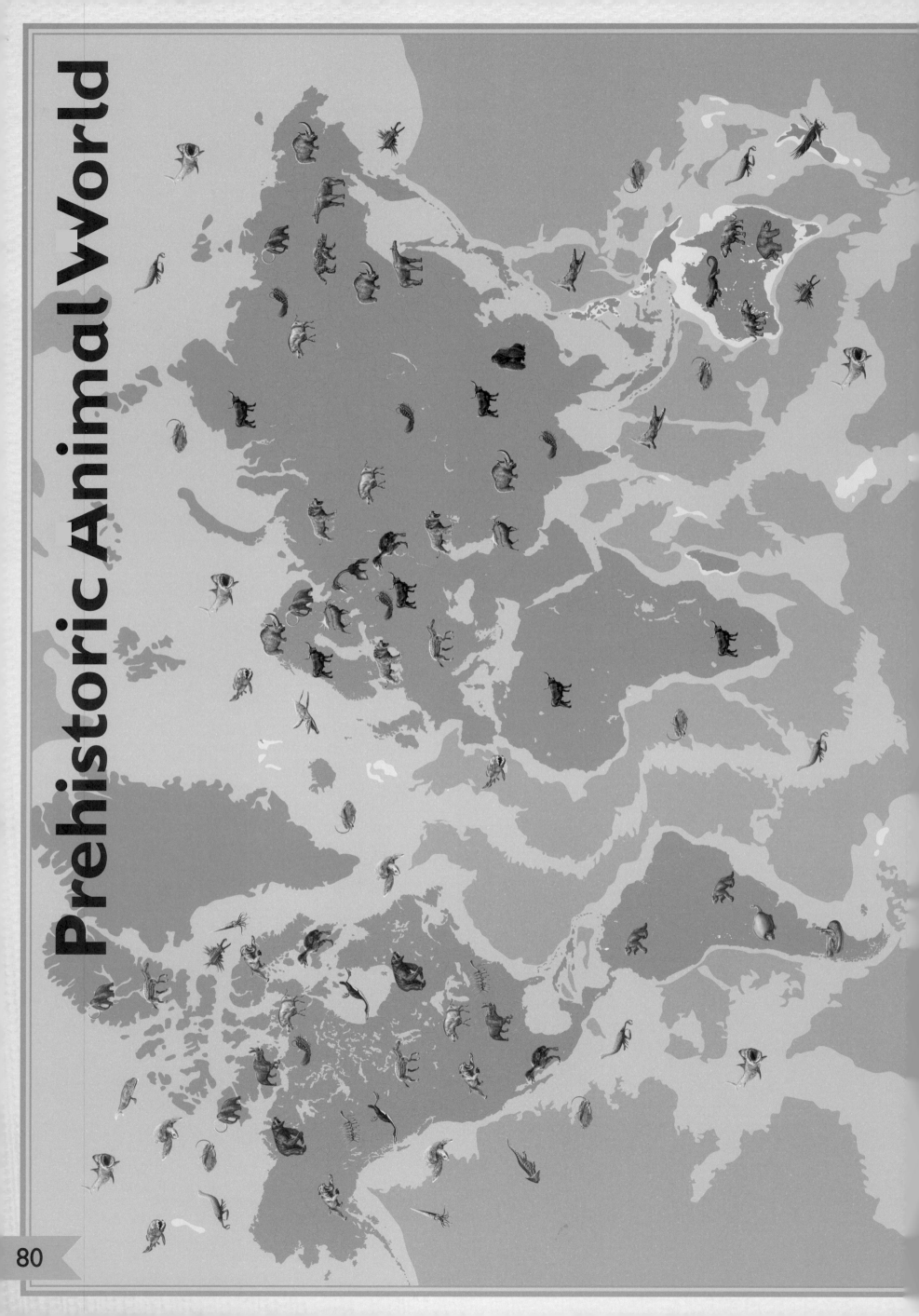